Praise for Danny Brassell, Ph.D.

"Dr. Danny Brassell is the kind of motivational speaker whose high energy, enthusiasm, and can-do spirit empowers teachers in ways to best serve English language learners and meet the needs of Every Child a Graduate by showing them how to effectively and affectively help students to develop both language acquisition and success in the content areas."

    - Mariah Adnane, CESA 7 Title III and ELL
    Coordinator
    Green Bay, Wisconsin

"Wonderful, outstanding and wacky...Danny Brassell is the first speaker that I have witnessed who can take what feels like a deck of cards that is stacked against you and reshuffles it in a way that motivates, relates and connects not just what but why and how to teach our diversified and challenging ELL population."

    - Elizabeth Harris, ELL Teacher
    Jonesborough, Tennessee

1

"Danny's presentation was an unforgettable, invaluable, and rewarding experience for me as an educator and parent. It was truly a meaningful, memorable and motivational choice of learning activities and interaction with the audience. His insights into the value and importance of reading were a powerful inspiration for me. Moreover, I was impressed at Danny's ability to capture his audience's attention from the very beginning to the very end, and get that emotional response only really gifted inspirational speakers possess. He is a difference maker."

> \- Lyudmyla Ziemke, ESOL Teacher,
> John F. Kennedy Middle School
> Riviera Beach, Florida

"Dr. Danny's presentations were engaging, full of energy and fun...but most importantly they were immediately useful for the classroom teacher."

> \- Richard P. Pierucci, Ed.D., Assoc.
> Superintendent, Norris School District
> Bakersfield, California

"Dr. Brassell is a dynamic and inspirational speaker. I had the pleasure of attending his presentations at the Tennessee Teachers of English to Speakers of Other Languages Conference this year. When you hear him speak, you are bombarded by ideas to enhance your teaching. He cuts right to the heart of the matter of how to reach students and get them to learn while enjoying themselves. I have already used several of his ideas in my own English classes at Vanderbilt University. Bravo Dr. Brassell!"

    - Michael Jumonville, Language Teaching
      Specialist, Vanderbilt University
      Nashville, Tennessee

"Dr. Brassell was fantastic! Our school in-service was the best one ever. Awesome. Our morale was down in the dumps – from the administration to every school in our district. Danny made me feel important again and reminded me that we all do make a difference each and every day, and – most of all – the kids need us. He is a must see. Love him. All I can say is 'WOW!'"

    - Lori Shannon, ELL Teacher
      Guymon, Oklahoma

"Thanks, Danny, for your enthusiastic presentation! It's two weeks since you've been here and people are still talking about what they've learned and how they're changing their classrooms."

- Debora Binkley, Ph.D., Associate Superintendent,
  Upper Arlington City Schools
  Upper Arlington, Ohio

"I can't thank Danny enough for providing the great opportunity of listening, participating and receiving such great information (too funny). What an inspiration and a breath of fresh air he is. He left us wanting more! Dr. Brassell reaffirmed that the basic foundation is what is lacking in many of today's classrooms/homes. When we talk about the 'bubble kids' and how we lose them along the way, it is us that have allowed it to happen."

- Rosalva Garza Larrasquitu,
  Parental Involvement Coordinator
  Brownsville, Texas

"Danny Brassell challenges even the most tenured teacher to take on the role of changing their behavior in the classroom. He gives participants a multitude of wonderful information to take back and use with students the very next day, which is precisely what adult learners want to do following an in-service presentation. I would unhesitatingly recommend Danny to any group that wants to learn new and exciting teaching strategies to use with the youngsters coming under their care."

- Hannah Worley, Ed.D., Training Facilitator
Macomb Intermediate School District
Clinton Township, Michigan

"Danny Brassell teaches us like we should be teaching our students. He combines practical and effective teaching strategies with pure, unadulterated fun! In one hour, I had learned a whole day's worth of ideas, and it only felt like 5 minutes. I would recommend Danny to anyone, regardless of the grade level or school. He's a real treat!"

-Kelly Epperson, ESL Teacher,
Unicoi County Schools
Erwin, Tennessee

"Danny was hired to provide our teachers with ways to differentiate instruction to reach all students including our growing ESL population. He did that and MORE! His presentations were energetic, interactive, and entertaining. Teachers came away with literally hundreds of ideas on how to reach students. He specifically focused on reading and writing with my staff. I can't imagine anyone more qualified to work with teachers in these areas."

- Derek Shouse, Principal, Saffell Street Elementary School, Lawrenceburg, Kentucky

"I teach in a Francophone High School, but we can always use Danny's material (even though it's in English). Danny is a true inspiration for us all. Today, in the middle of my grade 7 FLA class, we stood up and stretched and sang before continuing our class. It's great to see the immediate effect on the kids and their attention. I want to thank Danny for all of his practical ideas!"

- Chantal Desgagne, Teacher, Les Conseils Scolaires du Sud de l'Alberta, Calgary, Alberta, Canada

"Danny Brassell's presentation was the perfect fit for what my elementary school staff needed to hear about differentiated instruction given our large English learner population. His presentation was filled with practical strategies all teachers can implement immediately. Danny's presentation was as witty and fun as it was insightful and informative. I highly recommend him for any training you can possibly book since his energy level is contagious! Don't book this if you are looking for the typically dull and humorless training."

- Edward P. Fiszer, Ed.D., Principal, NEW Academy
Canoga Park, California

"Danny Brassell is a catalyst that inspires you to remember why we chose our teaching profession. His presentations are upbeat, entertaining, engaging, and focused on reading strategies that teachers can apply immediately. Danny has presented in our district on several occasions, and the teachers and principals beg to have him back."

- Jeanne Madere, Elementary English Language
Arts Consultant, Jefferson Parish P.S.S.
Harvey, Louisiana

"This was my second time in one of Danny's presentations, and I can say Danny inspired me once again! Keep doing what you are doing, Danny! He told us, 'we do not need to touch just one child; we need to touch every one of them.' I will tell you: Danny needs to keep touching every educator in this nation. God bless you, Danny!"

    - Julio Acevedo, Ed.S., Migrant Education
    Program/Title III Facilitator
    Lake Wales, Florida

"Hearing Danny Speak at the TNTESOL Conference was a 'teacher' moment for me! I was excited about returning to my ESL students and putting many of his amazing techniques and ideas into action. I also couldn't wait to discuss his techniques with supervisors and teachers alike. Danny 'gets it' when knowing how to logically go about helping a child learn to want and love to read. His ideas are not 'fly by night,' they are inspiring and will truly stand the test of time."

    - Sharon Lee, Assistant Principal/ESL Teacher
    Gibson County Special School District-Dyer School
    Dyer, Tennessee

"Danny Brassell is of the best motivational speakers for teachers and administrators ever! We left feeling energized and ready for the school year!"

- Carol Humphrey, Federal Programs Assistant
  Director, Raleigh County Schools
  Beckley, West Virginia

"Too often leaders are subjected to mundane presentations filled with bland and/or impertinent information. Danny has the unique ability to inspire while providing a lot of highly valuable information. I cannot wait to share his strategies with my staff."

- Stacy Murschel, Principal, Beulah Middle School
  Beulah, North Dakota

"Danny Brassell was a truly inspiring and entertaining speaker. He gave our ESL teachers strategies that they began utilizing right away. They thoroughly enjoyed his humor, wit and the information he shared with us. I received several emails about how much they appreciated the knowledge and insightfulness of the strategies that Danny presented to us. One teacher even requested that Danny return next year so that maybe 'Australian Pete' could speak (You have to have Danny come speak for your faculty to understand). It was a thoroughly enjoyable day."

     - Abasi McKinzie, Immigrant Facilitator,
     Shelby County Schools
     Memphis, Tennessee

"Best in-service I've been to...ever!"

     - Darcy Linn, Head Start Teacher,
     Franklin Elementary School
     Omaha, Nebraska

"...more than a workshop, more than a presentation – an educational event! Danny's energy and enthusiasm are awe inspiring, and if you're not inspired by what he has to say, you are in the wrong profession. Kids are first and foremost on his agenda and his ideas are powerful – a must see for all staff! Singing, dancing, and laughing – we can't be talking about school, or can we? With Danny Brassell at the helm, absolutely! I have rarely been to a more engaging professional development opportunity where I could actually bring back useful ideas to help my struggling and reluctant readers. A 'must see' if he is in your area!"

- Jack Costello, ELA Staff Development Specialist, Questar III BOCES Office
Castleton, New York

English
Language
LEARNERS

Understanding the English Language Learner:
Practical Tips to Boost Student Achievement

Danny Brassell, Ph.D.

America's Leading Reading Ambassador

Author of the Top-Selling Book
Bringing Joy Back into the Classroom

Printed in the United States of America

Library of Congress Control Number:

Brassell, Danny
Understanding the English Language Learner:
Practical Tips to Boost Student Achievement / by Danny Brassell
Library of Congress Cataloging-in-Publication Data
ISBN: 978-1-4675-6622-3

Danny Brassell

"America's Leading Reading Ambassador"

A few words of Motivation and Inspiration:

"Flexibility + Perseverance = results!"

"When parents, teachers and administrators are on the same page, it's a whole lot easier to get kids turning pages."

"It doesn't matter WHAT you read. What matters most is HOW MUCH you read."

"If you're not laughing, you're not learning."

"Leave your pride at the door, and do whatever it takes to make the people around you feel essential."

The Ideal Professional Speaker for Your Next Event!

To schedule Danny to Speak at Your Event:
(310) 872-9089 • www.dannybrassell.com

About Danny Brassell

America's leading reading ambassador, **DANNY BRASSELL** has delivered over 1,500 motivational presentations at conferences and meetings throughout North America. He is a professor in the Teacher Education Department at California State University-Dominguez Hills and founder of The Lazy Readers' Book Club (**www.lazyreaders.com**), Google's #1-ranked site for cool "short book recommendations." He is the author of over 50 journal and newspaper articles and 14 books, including *A Baker's Dozen of Lessons Learned from the Teaching Trenches*. Danny inspires people to read, lead and succeed, and he has conducted intensive personal and professional development seminars on leadership and success to thousands at over 1,000 corporations, school districts, universities, professional conferences and conventions.

Danny has taught students ranging from preschoolers to rocket scientists, and he has worked with some of the world's leading literacy experts. During his time as a classroom teacher, reading tutor, non-profit leader, professor, educational administrator, salesman and business owner, Danny has incorporated his "reading secrets" philosophy to great avail.

Today, Danny shares his incredible 20+ years of education experiences and success model to empower leaders, teams and audiences to achieve extraordinary results. Danny's keynotes and presentations have earned a reputation for being high energy, (sometimes theatrical) enthusiastic, creative, applicable and highly motivating.

For more resources and to subscribe to Danny's
FREE "Success Tips" e-zine newsletter,
visit **www.dannybrassell.com**

Engage and Inspire Your Students!

Have you ever seen an inspirational movie about a teacher who is handed the toughest class, only to win the hearts and souls of students by utilizing the school's mandated textbook program? Neither have I.

What happens when you are given gobs and gobs of learning standards and scripted lesson plans with little or no attention to how to engage students? Too many teachers enter the profession fantasizing of attentive students who find everything they say captivating, only to find that the realities of many classrooms are students who are bored, under-motivated and disinterested in school. Combine that with greater numbers of students entering classrooms with limited or no English language proficiency, and it is a wonder teachers manage to teach students anything at all.

I've been there, and I greatly value the challenges you face as a teacher. Whether you are in the classroom or at central office, at home or at the office, I'd like to share with you a variety of engaging ways you can make learning fun and long-lasting for your English language learners. This book offers simple suggestions that will help you engage and inspire your English language learner students and help them produce greater results than ever before!

- Danny Brassell, Ph.D.

Motivate and Inspire Others! "Share This Book"

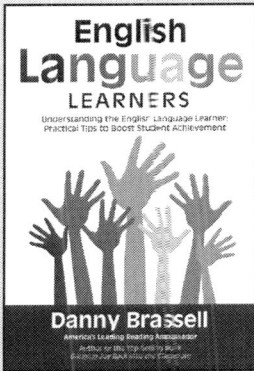

Understanding the English Language Learner: Practical Tips to Boost Student Achievement

All teachers need quick and handy tricks to engage their students. Whether you're dealing with kindergartners or 12th graders, teaching English Language Learners with limited English or none at all – this resource is designed to equip you with awesome tools to involve students in meaningful ways that are sure to produce greater results in your classroom! $29.97

Special Quantity Discounts

10-20	Books	$27.00	each
21-99	Books	$24.00	each
100-499	Books	$18.00	each
500-999	Books	$13.00	each
1,000+	Books	$8.00	each

www.dannybrassell.com

Introduction

Say Hello!

I always start my classes with songs and chants, so for this "scat," you need to ask students to get out of their seats and follow you like cars of a train or a mamba line. It is to the rhythm of *Scat Like That*, and if you haven't the foggiest notion what that sounds like, the only thing you have to know is to make your voice gravelly and ask students to repeat everything you say. The origin and non-phonetic spelling of each foreign language word for hello is provided in italics beside the pronunciation. Now get up, and lead your students:

Ho-la. (hola, Spanish)
Oh-see-YOH! (osiyo, Cherokee)
Nah-mah-STAY. (namaste, Hindi)
Koh-NEE-cheewah! (konichiwa, Japanese)

(chorus)
Say "hello."
I said, "Say Hello!"
Say "hello."
I said, "Say Hello!"
Sha-LOHM. (shalom, Hebrew)
Nee HaOW! (nihao, Mandarin)
Bohn-ZHOOR. (bonjour, French)
GOOT-en Tahk! (guten tag, German)

Repeat the chorus twice, fading away and sitting on the second chorus. Are you pumped to learn more ways to have a positive impact working with your ELL students? Let's get this book started!

ESL, ELL & Other Abbreviations

ESL, ELL, ESOL – what on Earth are we talking about? The field of education has no shortage of abbreviations and acronyms, and our educational jargon can sometimes resemble the jargon reserved for the military, truck drivers and police officers (breaker, breaker – what's your 20?).

ESL, or English as a Second Language, is the common abbreviation used in some states. Others prefer to deem students as "English Language Learners," or ELLs. ESOL is the acronym for teaching "English to Speakers of Other Languages." I have even seen some Districts use the abbreviation "CLD" students for their "culturally and linguistically diverse" population, which I particularly like because it acknowledges that many students who are learning English may not come from foreign language backgrounds. Regardless, can we agree to not get wound up over which abbreviation I choose to use throughout this text? What is appropriate for Florida may not be the vernacular of California. For the sake of consistency, I have chosen to stick with ELL students (although it is entirely possible that I slip and insert English as a Second Language from time to time). Breathe in; breathe out. We'll get through this.

Teaching Framework

Let's face it: learning English ain't easy. It is not easy to teach, either. Some teachers may encounter a class with all native Spanish speakers. Others have students from various language backgrounds scattered throughout their classrooms. It can be overwhelming, to say the least!

When I first began teaching my ELL students, I felt like Charlie Chaplin. Put simply, I was gesturing like a madman. Often I would repeat myself louder, as if I were teaching deaf students rather than ELL students. I quickly learned, too, that having students copy down information or repeat it back to me served little purpose when I provided little or no context based on my students' own experiences. It quickly became apparent to me that I needed to let my students guide my instruction, not vice versa. This may appear more difficult for teachers facing new students year-in and year-out, but nobody ever said good teaching was easy.

Good teachers follow a broad plan, recognizing that all students are different and enter classrooms with varying degrees of language proficiency, content knowledge and family backgrounds. The following principles should be considered in guiding students' English language development:

- Create a comfortable, low-anxiety environment that supports students by promoting risk-taking and interaction
- Build on students' prior background knowledge
- Demonstrate and model everything, always providing students with clear expectations
- Use language in meaningful contexts (e.g., use gestures, incorporate manipulatives, etc.)
- Differentiate instruction based on students' learning styles and interests
- Maintain high expectations and provide all students with the support and tools they need to achieve
- Incorporate subject matter with language development whenever possible

- Remember: school and fun do not have to be mutually exclusive
- Keep it simple, silly! Rome wasn't built in a day.

ELL students are some of the most patient and forgiving people I have ever known. I have classes endure my rapid speech, tendency to talk off-topic and a variety of other personal failings. They teach me just as much as I teach them, if not more. Along the way I have picked up a variety of strategies to help make my lessons easier to understand, including:

- Slow down! The faster you talk, the more likely you're going to stare at a bunch of blank faces in your classroom.
- Try to use high-frequency vocabulary rather than technical terms.
- Remember that communication is the major goal of language. Encourage students whenever they successfully communicate a concept (e.g., I once had a student say airplane driver. While pilot may be a more specific term, did that student communicate

his point to me? Of course! In many ways learning a second language is one of the best mental creativity exercises we can practice.).

- Pause often. It gives you a chance to catch your breath and students a chance to translate.
- Enunciate clearly.
- Use lots of gestures, facial expressions, manipulatives (realia) to provide further context for students.
- Check for understanding throughout your lessons. Don't wait for the end, and fall into the "Does everybody understand?" trap, as more often than not your students will nod their heads without demonstrating any comprehension of your lesson.
- Use nouns rather than pronouns. It makes it easier for listeners to understand who, what or where you are specifically talking about, rather than getting lost in "pronoun world." By the way – I teach this as a habit for my native English-speaking students, as well.
- Vary your styles of delivery, remembering that students learn in different ways. Some prefer information to be presented visually, while others like to listen to lessons. Still others prefer to move

while they learn. Accommodate accordingly.

- Avoid idiomatic expressions as much as possible, as the English language is loaded with expressions that may be familiar to native speakers but pile unnecessary stress and confusion on ELL students. Of course, make sure to review idiomatic expressions (my classes always play a variety of idiom games to familiarize themselves with our often kooky sayings).

- Provide as many opportunities for students to interact with one another as possible. The best teacher in the ELL classroom is usually not the person standing in the front of the class. Rather, students tend to do a better job teaching one another (Lev Vygotsky would argue this is an example of your "zone of proximal development," but we'll save that discussion for another time).

- Encourage students like a coach. Coaches constantly provide their players feedback. We need to do a lot less assessing and labeling of students and a lot more coaching of students.

- Remember: school and fun do not have to be mutually exclusive

- Keep it simple, silly! Rome wasn't built in a day.
- Repeat and reinforce.
- Repeat and reinforce.
- Repeat and reinforce.

A wise professor from Harvard once said that, "We hear a book a day. Speak a book a week. Read a book a month. And write a book a year." What he means by that is that typical Americans hear the equivalent of an adult novel in everyday situations. To accomplish the same feat, it takes most Americans approximately a week to speak an adult novel, a month to read one and a year to write one. Translation: while there are four elements of language acquisition (listening, speaking, reading, writing), listening plays the most prominent role. That is why teachers should not fear ELL students who choose not to speak. Everyone goes through a "silent period" when acquiring a second language.

Goals of This Book

Too many academic texts sit on shelves, never to be utilized by classroom teachers. If I have done my job, this book should be highlighted, bent out of shape and loaded with coffee stains. I want you to use this book. It is designed to be short and sweet and filled with the gems that have aided me when teaching my ELL students.

So, by the end of this book, we will have:

1. Examined how to apply language acquisition theory in practical ways that benefit ELL students on a daily basis;

2. Reviewed ways to create a classroom environment that ensures high interest in learning among ELL students; and

3. Discussed how to promote a variety of vocabulary enhancement tricks to build on ELL students' prior knowledge and interests.

ELL Background

Pop Quiz

Nothing gets people more excited than a pop quiz, right? In a test-consumed environment that sees accountability simply as the number of "correct" answers on a one-shot exam, it is a wonder more ELL teachers don't begin talking to themselves. Let's look at what you know about ELL students with this three-question, multiple-choice quiz.

Question 1: What does "ELL" refer to?
a) a rock band from the 1970s with electric violins
b) the latest popular street drug
c) English Language Learners

Take a moment and consult a neighbor to determine an answer. If you answered "c," that is what the judges were looking for, so you are already well on your way to success.

Question 2: Who are ELL students?
a) Congress
b) Hollywood
c) learners whose primary language is not English, yet who live in places where English has some sort of special status or public availability

When in doubt, Harvard studies have shown that "c" is the best answer. By the way, the judges would have accepted "a" or "b," as well. Time for one final question:

Question 3: What is the largest group of ELL students?
a) professional athletes
b) smokers
c) Hispanic/Latino and Asian/Pacific Islander

If you answered "c," you are well on your way to success as an ELL teacher. By the way – it should be pointed out that at different times in American history, ELL students have come from a variety of places – from Ireland to Italy, Russia to Africa. What's my point? We are a nation of immigrants, and unless your ancestors were native Americans, it is a pretty good idea to recognize how important our immigrant population has been to the development and prosperity of our country.

Factors Affecting ELL Students

Age. Who do you think learns a second language more easily, children or adults? If you answered "children," you would be absolutely wrong. As one of my mentors, Dr. Stephen Krashen, of the University of Southern California points out: children acquire a second language more easily. Adults learn a second language more easily. We'll dive deeper into that later.

Personality. Who do you think learns a second language more easily, shy students or outgoing students? If you said "outgoing students," you need to know that there is no research to prove one or the other. Just because a student sits in the front row and raises her hand incessantly does not necessarily mean she is learning more than the shy "Unabomber" in the back of the class that never says a word. In fact, often the student who is quiet learns more than the more talkative student because his ears are open and mouth is shut.

Environment. Who do you think learns a second language more easily, students with access to lots of resources or students with limited resources? This question is not a trick. The student who has access to lots of resources has a distinct advantage over the student with limited access to materials, so we must strive as educators to provide our ELL students with as many language enhancement tools as possible.

The Secret to Teaching ELL Students
Here is a gem that will make you a better teacher: what's good for ELL students is good for all students. We are

blessed to teach ELL students. All students are different. All students have special needs. We need to embrace the diversity of our classrooms rather than strive for homogeneity.

True, ELL students are different. For one, they don't speak English as well as native English speakers. Have you ever noticed that? Additionally, they come to our classrooms with varying degrees of language proficiency. For example, when I used to teach international students at the University of Southern California's American Language Institute, one of my duties was to test incoming international students for their degrees of English language proficiency. For example, I'd ask them what they were studying, and a more proficient student might go on and on about his engineering program. Often these students spoke excellent English but were self conscious about their accents (something that I never understood, as I have always enjoyed the sounds of different accents, and a former governor of ours in California had a pretty thick accent and did pretty well for himself). Meanwhile, other students would just nod at any questions I asked and say "yes." This is an indicator that the student could use some language assistance.

Additionally, our ELL students come to us with varying language backgrounds. Spanish is quite different from Farsi, and German varies quite a bit from Mandarin. Being familiar with language backgrounds can assist ELL teachers who are trying to better understand student difficulties (e.g., often Spanish speakers will place adjectives after nouns, as Spanish emphasizes the noun before the adjective). While considering the language backgrounds of ELL students, it is also a good idea to grasp varying cultural backgrounds of students. Two words that have served me well are "I'm sorry." I have made a ton of mistakes based on my own cultural assumptions (e.g., I asked a student to look at me when I spoke to him, only to discover that in his culture it is a sign of respect not to look into the eyes of the teacher). A sincere apology can go a long way in building trust.

Duh, you say? You want to know specifically what you can do to help your ELL students. I have three ideas. First, we need to be "AWARE." AWARE stands for

"Always Watch out for Administrators Roaming and Evaluating." Let's not let standards and mandates interfere with our teaching. Second, we need to "CARE." CARE stands for creating a "Comfortable Atmosphere and Relaxed Environment." Our ELL students will learn English quicker when they feel at ease with their teachers and classmates. Finally, we need to "SHARE." SHARE stands for "Supply Hordes of Amazing Resources in our Environments." What materials do we provide our students that will make them learn English quicker and more easily?

Krashen's Five Hypotheses

One of my mentors at the University of Southern California was Stephen Krashen, considered to be one of the world's foremost authorities on second language acquisition. Krashen developed five central hypotheses to explain how ELL students develop their second language proficiency. He developed these hypotheses about second language acquisition in order to assist classroom second language learning. Krashen's five hypotheses (in no particular order) are: (1) the affective filter hypothesis; (2) the natural order hypothesis; (3)

the acquisition-learning hypothesis; (4) the monitor hypothesis; and (5) the input hypothesis. While there are other language acquisition theories, this book builds upon Krashen's model.

The Affective Filter Hypothesis. Krashen uses the fancy term "affective filter" to address the second language learner's social-emotional variables: one's anxiety. The higher the affective filter, the greater the anxiety. Learners acquire language more easily when they are relaxed, motivated to learn the language and confident in themselves. Listening, Krashen argues, is the most essential ingredient to second language acquisition, so teachers should allow ELL students a "silent period" when they are allowed to focus on listening and understanding, as opposed to rote memorization and drill-and-kill.

The Natural Order Hypothesis. Krashen argues that it does not matter if you are born in Boston or Bangladesh, all learners acquire language in a predictable order. One does not come out of the womb requesting a blanket, and one does not pick up a second language overnight.

The Acquisition-Learning Hypothesis. The easiest way I know to convey Krashen's thoughts concerning language acquisition-learning differences is this: language is thought, and learning is taught. When a student acquires a language he does it effortlessly. It is a subconscious process. Meanwhile, learning is a conscious process. As adults have had more experience developing learning strategies, they have a conscious "learning" advantage over children.

The Monitor Hypothesis. If you had a friend who wanted to learn German, what would you suggest she do? You'd probably recommend she go to Germany, not take a basic German language class at a local college. Krashen's monitor hypothesis, however, recommends that basic language course before the trip, as he claims it will train the learner's ear (thus allowing the learner to acquire more German on her trip to Germany). Krashen suggests that the formal study of language leads to the development of an internal grammar editor (monitor). Sufficient time, focus on grammatical form and explicit knowledge of rules are essential to the monitor, making it easier to use the monitor when writing a language than speaking it. Learners benefit from a minimum language "threshold."

The Input Hypothesis. I know I said there was no order to these hypotheses, but I saved the best for last. Krashen argues that we learn language in one way – and one way only: when we understand the message. We understand languages through cues like gestures, building on background experiences, providing realia, etc., and these tools for language assistance provide students with "comprehensible input." The "teacher," one who is more competent in the target language, provides the "student" with language that contains grammatical structures that are just a bit beyond the student's current level of second language development (Krashen called this i + 1, where i stands for input and +1 indicates the challenging level that is a bit beyond the student's current level of proficiency).

Russian educational theorist Lev Vygotsky believed that children learn to engage in higher-level thinking by learning first how to communicate (through listening, speaking, reading and writing). The more your ELL students can use language in the classroom, the more they will learn how to think. Good ELL teachers allow their students to communicate in their first language en route to a better understanding of communication skills in their second language. The following sections of this book will focus on specific activities you may facilitate in your classroom to promote your ELL students' English language development.

Listening and Speaking

Listening and speaking skills are essential building blocks to ELL students' mastery of English as a second language. Educator and researcher Walter Loban once said, "We listen to the equivalent of a book a day, talk the equivalent of a book a week, read the equivalent of a book a month, and write the equivalent of a book a year." Loban wanted to emphasize the dominant role that oral language plays in everyday experiences. Additionally, Loban pled, "Please – in the name of all that is good in language and thinking, please let the children talk. Let them talk a great deal."

Children need to learn how to listen as well. The development of speaking and listening skills must continue from preschool throughout a student's academic career. Oral language development must not be discounted in the classroom, as loud classrooms are learning classrooms. Oral language provides the foundation for thinking in and about language. A significant link exists between well-developed oral language and strong reading and writing skills. Thus, developed listening and speaking skills provide the gateway to better reading and writing skills.

The classroom is a natural environment for a large variety of language learning opportunities, and good ELL teachers can organize their classrooms in ways that encourage the two most important elements of oral language development: comprehensible input and social interaction.

Predictable routines are critical for the success of any classroom, especially one filled with ELL students. A predictable schedule empowers students to adjust to the classroom and provides easily acquired basic vocabulary with repeated routines. Besides attendance, recess, lunch and dismissal, the use of routine instructional events also provides oral language learning opportunities. Some typical routine instructional events include morning meeting, journals, literature circles, process writing, service-based learning projects, thematic units, etc. Familiar language improves student participation and learning. Routines in the classroom provide the same comfort audiences find in the predictability of movies with their favorite action stars.

Whether you are engaging your students in literature circles, morning meetings or service-based learning projects, it is always important to review your own instructional delivery to incorporate additional cues to convey meaning, especially nonverbal cues, such as dramatization, gestures, pictures, graphic organizers and realia. Good ELL teachers are reflective practitioners, constantly thinking of better ways to reach all of their students. Beyond managerial and instructional routines, there are a number of wonderful learning activities that showcase oral language use in ways that promote acquisition. Because they provide opportunities for negotiation of meaning through social interaction, they facilitate oral language development.

Games. Games are good. Always remember that. Whether you use simulation games or pronunciation games, story games or grammar games, games improve student learning and create an atmosphere of ease, creativity and, yes, fun. School and fun do not have to be mutually exclusive.

Songs and Chants. Use music and chants in the class. These activities are motivating for students and also help teach English pronunciation and intonation patterns. Songs and chants assist students in remembering concepts, too. To get students "in the mood" for a topic, listen to a song. Repetition and group recitation, in my experience, are powerful ways to encourage students to participate in non-threatening ways.

Drama. Acting out stories and events in various curricular areas can be a highly motivating way for students to process and present information they have studied. These activities can range from the informal to formal, but good ELL teachers ensure a non-threatening environment where students are encouraged to take risks. Dramatic activities are easily differentiated, as beginning ELL students could be encouraged to pantomime events, intermediate students could create their own skits ahead of time and more advanced students could be asked to improvise little plays of their own on the spot. Dramatic activities provide students with a variety of contextualized and scaffolded activities that gradually involve more participation and more oral language proficiency.

Poetry. Why use poetry with ELL students? Why not! Poems are succinct; they are a lot shorter to read aloud, making them less intimidating than regular books and stories. Poetry enables students to discover the power of words and expand their English vocabularies. Poetry can be effectively used to help students understand common homonyms (e.g., to, two, too). Poetry uses rhythm to highlight or emphasize specific words, and it is very useful in reinforcing content. Finally, the cultural aspects of poetry should never be underestimated when working with ELL students, as good ELL teachers include poems that are familiar to students' home cultures.

In summary, there are a variety of oral language development opportunities available in the ELL classroom through games, songs and chants, drama and poetry (by the way, these are only the starting points for quality instruction). The activities described in this section facilitate oral language development in at least three ways: (1) they encourage students to work in groups on motivating projects; (2) they provide various scaffolds for oral language performance, allowing ELL students of all ability levels to participate; and (3) they focus on fun uses of oral language, reducing the anxiety sometimes associated with using a second language. Here are a variety of activities my past ELL students have enjoyed:

Alphabet Stoop
Tell students you are going to create an "alphabet story" together. Begin the story with the letter "A" (e.g., I met an architect on an airplane.). If possible (but not necessary), ask a student whose name begins with that letter to add a sentence with the letter "B" (e.g., I bought him a burger.). Continue all the way to the end of the alphabet. If a student has difficulty, encourage the class to brainstorm words that start with a given letter.

Barrier Games

Give pairs of students a screen or board to act as a barrier between them (three sides of a cardboard box can be used effectively) and two identical game boards and/or sets of identical objects. Next, ask students to set up their barriers so that they may place and identify the objects on their game boards without being observed by their partners. The first student selects an object and describes it to the partner. The student then places it on the game board, describing the location to the partner. The partner selects the object matching the description from an identical collection and places it on the position that the first student described. The first student continues to describe and place objects until a selection or all objects are placed. The students remove the barrier and compare their arrangements. The object of the game is to match both sides exactly. Tell students to discuss differences and similarities between their game boards.

Character Hot Seat

Read aloud a story to the class, and ask a student volunteer to impersonate a character from the story.

Allow students to ask the student volunteer questions about the story. Student volunteer gets to share answers from point of view of her character.

Class Brainstorm

Given a particular topic, gather students' ideas and thoughts on whiteboard. Remind students the rules of class brainstorms: there are no bad ideas. Students randomly share their ideas based on the topic of discussion, as you record their responses. This is an easy activity that can be used to preview lessons, stimulate writing ideas, etc.

Collage

As a class, decide on a theme. Students use newspapers or magazines as resources and cut out pictures or captions that are related to the identified theme. Finally, students share their collages with the class and give oral presentations about their collages.

Daily Phrase Passwords

Teach the class about useful everyday phrases (i.e. May I go to the restroom?, My name is _____, How are you?,

How do you say _____, etc.). Post each phrase with a visual to help students remember it (and you can even ask students to illustrate the visuals). Students must recall and use the phrase to be able to leave the class for lunch, dismissal, etc. In the beginning you may want to teach one per day (as well as review past day phrases).

Draw & Tell

Ask students to each draw a picture that is related to the theme the class is learning, and allow each student volunteer to share her drawing with the class. Guide students through telling the class about their pictures by asking them to describe their picture's color and details.

Electric Slide

Students stand in a line. First student says a word or phrase and provides a movement or gesture (e.g., tug on ear, stomp a foot, etc.). The next student repeats it and adds a word or phrase of her own, along with a movement or unique gesture. Repeat all the way to final student, and then review as a group everyone's unique word/phrase and movement/gesture.

End-of-Day Kudos

I observed a second grade teacher in Tokyo who saved the last ten minutes of each day for students to stand up and praise other students who helped them throughout the day. Wow! What a great way to end the school day and foster teamwork among your ELL students.

Find Your Way

Create a classroom maze (you can put masking tape on the floor, rearrange desks, etc.). Blindfold a student. Other students will make a statement using one of four sentences: declarative (makes a statement.); interrogative (asks a question?); imperative (gives a command or makes a request.!); or exclamatory (expresses strong feeling!). Blindfolded student listens to sentence and takes a step forward for a declarative sentence, to the left for an interrogative sentence, to the right for an imperative sentence and backward for an exclamatory sentence. The goal is for the class to help guide the blindfolded student to the target destination and for all students to learn about four types of sentences.

Flannel Board Story

Tell a story using a flannel board and flannel cut-out characters (if you don't have a flannel board/cut-out characters, then use a white board and cardboard cut-out characters). As you tell the story, students place each character cut-out on the board. Ask students to identify the characters in a variety of ways, such as pointing and providing short answers. Ask students to retell the story or create a new story using the same characters. Please note: you can use this activity across subject areas (e.g., instead of a story, you could present students with concepts such as counting, addition and subtraction).

Four Corners

Choose a topic that you can survey students opinions' on, asking students to move to the appropriate corner if they: (1) strongly agree with a statement; (2) agree with a statement; (3) strongly disagree with a statement; or (4) disagree with a statement. Once in their corners, students pair with other students to discuss why they chose that corner and prepare to share with the group.

Great Performances

Select volunteers for actors and actresses to portray characters in a story. Make sure to give students necessary props. While the class is listening to the story being played on tape or being read aloud by you, performers act out the story. Students can re-enact the story several times, and you may ask students to take turns being the narrator.

Guessing Game

Place an object inside a bag and ask students to stick their arms inside. Hold the bag so that students may not see the object. Each student takes a turn and comes up with a descriptive word about the object. Other students create a word list and, based on descriptors, guess what the object is.

Hand Signals

To encourage nonverbal participation among beginning ELL students, teach hand signals for agree/disagree (e.g., thumbs up/thumbs down), questions (e.g., students curl index fingers in air), degree of understanding (e.g., 1-4 fingers from low to high/fist for no understanding), etc.

Hot Square

Designate an area in your classroom known as the "hot square." ELL students know that when I stand in the Hot Square, they absolutely need to pay attention because the information is critical. Some folks tell me, "Well, everything I tell students is critical." I'd beg to differ. Figure out your priorities and direct students' attention to them by standing in the Hot Square. Once your ELL students get the hang of it, they can stand there whenever they have something important to say to you (or the class).

Human Clock

Twelve students stand in a circle forming a clock, each holding a number from 1 to 12. In the center of the circle, two students represent the big hand and little hand on the clock and point to different times that either you or a student volunteer calls out.

Human Typewriter

Prepare a set of flashcards, and randomly pass out a card to each student. Pick a word from your list and ask student with that word to say his word and spell it out orally. Then, ask student to write his name in the air. On the floor of your classroom, place letters of alphabet, arranged like the letters on a keyboard. Ask student to "hop-spell" his word on the typewriter.

Bonus: afterward, you can also ask student to "channel his inner-Village Person," and spell his word with his body "Y-M-C-A-style."

Imitate the Teacher

If you have the guts, have a contest to see which of your students can impersonate you the best. It will scare you how many of your habits students pick up. I am convinced that humans should not be called homo sapiens. Rather, we should be called homo imitatus. We have an amazing ability to imitate those around us, and this activity will serve you well as a teacher trying to determine what your students are learning.

K-W-L+

As a class, make a list of topics of interest (students dictate as you write on whiteboard). Through class discussion, one topic is chosen. As a class, fill-in the parts of a "K-W-L+" concept map by identifying What We Know and What We Want to Know. Explore possible resources to answer sections of What We Want to Know using various processes (e.g., direct teaching, books, interviews, research, etc.). Hold a presentation of findings using various products (e.g., role play, news report, panel discussions, podcasts, etc.). Afterward, discuss What We Have Learned and What We Still Want to Learn for another theme cycle.

Lunch Line Shakes

Never waste a minute of your day. There are constant opportunities to promote language among your ELL students. In movie theaters it is said that "silence is golden." Well, "silence is deadly" for ELL students. They need to hear and use as much English as possible. So use every moment of your time with students as an opportunity for them to hear and use language. For example, when my students and I stood in lunch lines outside the cafeteria, I would lead the students in chants and songs. After you model this behavior, students can eventually lead the activity. You will be amazed how quickly your students will pick up a fair amount of English in this way.

Mystery Box

Place something in a box prior to beginning the lesson. Students ask questions to help them guess what is inside the box. You may respond with only "yes" or "no" to the questions asked. Tip: try to choose something that relates to the lesson you are going to present, as that will provide automatic interest and curiosity about the lesson.

Name Game

This is an activity for the class to become acquainted. Students pass an object around and each student says his name upon receiving the object. The first person says the name of the person to whom he is going to give the object. The second person says her name with an adjective beginning with the same letter. The second person then says the name of the person to whom the object will be given, etc. (e.g., My name is Ahmed. Lucia. My name is Lucia, lovely Lucia. Priyanka. My name is Priyanka, pretty Priyanka. Victor. My name is Victor, valient Victor.).

Oral History

Ask students to tell their own stories and the stories of their families.

Pantomime

Prepare six to eight short sentences describing a sequence of actions in a specific context. Then collect or create visuals and props to accompany each action. Act out the sentences using visuals and props while clearly saying the sentences. Students respond in pantomime, first in groups and then on their own. Stop modeling the actions and ask students to orally respond to the sentences. Students now imitate the sentences as well as the actions. For example, you could review what students are to do when they come to class: 1. I enter the room; 2. I go to my seat; 3. I sit down; 4. I take out my book; 5. I take out my pencil; 6. I greet my teacher.

Preference Ranking

Select a topic and survey students' preferences. The topic may be food, colors, friends, hobbies – whatever. Introduce key vocabulary words and use a chart to record the results of the survey. Then, ask students questions based on the survey, and feel free to modify the questions for students' varying language proficiency levels (e.g., Point to the most popular food in class. What is the most popular food in our class?

Why do you think cheeseburgers are the most popular?).

Preview with a Partner
Distribute a pretest (which should be very similar to a posttest) and one pencil to each pair of students, and ask them to pass the pretest and pencil back and forth. Students alternate reciting questions aloud, and partners discuss possible answers.

Readers' Theatre
Prepare a set of scripts for student volunteers. You may want to use a script that has some repetition of phrases or follows a pattern (e.g., the first person said...the second person said...etc.). Ask volunteers to stand in front of the class with their backs to the audience (you can also ask students to stand behind a white board/ cardboard box and use puppets to speak their parts). When it is time for student volunteers to read their parts, they may face the audience or reveal their puppets to the audience. Once a volunteer reads his line, he can turn away from the audience again. Make sure students are allowed opportunities to practice with one another before performing in front of the class.

Scavenger Hunt

Create a list of questions or statements prior to this activity. Give the list of questions to each student. Students have to find people in the class who can answer the questions and then sign their names on the question sheet. Students have to find a different person for each item on the list (e.g., has a brother or sister, hates tests, goes to bed by 9 p.m., etc.). Note: you may also use this activity to review key concepts in content subjects.

Songs, Rhymes & Chants

Teach students a variety of songs, rhymes and chants with actions. This is also a great way to introduce students to songs, rhymes and chants popularly known in America and integrates songs, rhymes and chants from students' home cultures. Students can clap, follow the rhythms and act out the actions.

Sorting

Prepare objects or picture cards with several different themes. Then, mix up the objects or picture cards. Introduce vocabulary words for each category (e.g., seasons, types of animals, types of food, classroom items, etc.). Students sort the objects or picture cards into the appropriate categories and briefly state the reasons for their choices.

Sound Effects

Play different recorded sounds from the environment aloud on an audiotape. Students listen to the sounds and identify them by discussing with a partner. Partners then draw and/or write the word. Students can also create sounds and ask classmates to guess what each sound is.

Speed Dating

Instruct students to stand in two straight lines, Line A and Line B, facing each other (each line has the same number of students). Students in Line A ask the student facing them in Line B a question, then student in Line B answers question. The first student in Line A moves to the end of the line (students in Line B stay where they are), and everyone else in Line A moves up a space. Repeat rotation after each question. Students in Line A ask new partner another question.

Think-Pair-Share

Pose a question that generates students' opinions. Students think of their answers on their own (they may write notes, if they wish), and then they share their opinions with partners. Each pair shares their responses with another pair. Ask volunteers to share their answers with the class.

Walk the Line

Place tape down the center of the classroom. Ask students yes/no, true/false, either/or questions where they have to choose to stand on one side or the other. Give students time to think about their choices and share their reasons with a partner. Ask student volunteers to share their reasons with the class.

Reading

Literacy is power. The ability to read is critical, especially for ELL students. Besides listening to native speakers, one of the best ways students can acquire English vocabulary is through extensive reading.

A reader who speaks English as a second language uses essentially the same process that a native speaker uses to read a passage. Yet the task can be considerably more difficult. Why?

Well, important differences in language proficiency and background knowledge pertinent to the text being read play a significant role in what the reader understands. For example, a student from Saudi Arabia may have limited knowledge of *Goldilocks and the Three Bears*. A key vocabulary term such as porridge can be difficult enough for native speakers to grasp, let alone an ELL student. Exposure to predictable patterns can greatly assist students (e.g., Once upon a time).

In recent years, researchers have looked at how people process print when reading English as a second language. They consistently find that the process is essentially the same whether reading English as the first or second language. In other words, both first and second language readers look at the page and the print and use their knowledge of sound/symbol relationships, word order, grammar and meaning to predict and confirm meaning. As they read, readers use their background knowledge about the text's topic and structure along with their linguistic knowledge and reading strategies in order to interpret what they read. If their interpretation does not make sense, they go back and read it again.

Reading can provide a wide range of language input (context) unavailable to ELL students in other ways. Through reading, ELL students can virtually "peek" into the lives and cultures of native speakers, and they can experience a much wider variety of conversational situations than they would through their own interactions with native speakers. Reading is also an excellent means of vocabulary and grammar development.

Like listening, reading involves constructing meaning. Many researchers have observed that reading in a second language corresponds closely to reading in a first language. The major differences ELL students encounter between reading in a second language as opposed to in their native language involve the greater number of unknown vocabulary words and language forms ELL students encounter. Their background knowledge and degree of language proficiency play a significant role in their comprehension of what they read. For example, when people read in their first language, they have already developed their language ability – which allows them to recognize words they are sounding out relatively easily. In a second language, however, many of the words may still seem unfamiliar even if sounded out correctly.

Additionally, grammatical features – such as verb endings and word order – are less useful in helping to understand a second language reading text. As a result, many scholars believe that a minimum "threshold" level of language ability is necessary before true second language reading can occur (translation: re-read Krashen's monitor hypothesis). Until ELL students have developed an adequate amount of internalized second language ability, they are more likely to translate rather than draw meaning directly from text. Building ELL students' familiarity with topics is critical in assisting them in their comprehension of various vocabulary and situations.

Teachers must appreciate the complexity of English that faces many of their ELL students, as students also often have to deal with the difficulty of learning a new alphabet. Many languages do not share a common alphabet, and even when the native language and English use the same alphabet (e.g., Spanish), a new set of sound-symbol correspondences must be learned. As a result, ELL students will see a letter used in their native language and have to learn to think of a different sound or sounds when they see that letter used in a written text. New alphabets typically pose even greater challenges for ELL students. English-speaking learners of languages like Russian, Greek, Korean, Arabic, Hebrew and Farsi must learn entirely new scripts, and learners of certain Asian languages such as Mandarin and Japanese must cope with the intricacies of character-based writing systems. Some languages, such as Japanese, require the mastery of multiple alphabets. And the grammatical structures of languages may vary, as well (e.g., in Spanish, adjectives proceed nouns).

In conclusion, it is vital that ELL teachers are aware of the challenges their students face in acquiring English. The activities described in this section facilitate language development through reading in a number of ways. Want to know my best tip for you? Let your ELL students choose whatever they want to read, talk to them about what they are reading and give them plenty of access and opportunities to read. Here are a few other activities to add to your bag of tricks:

Analogies

Select familiar words from a text. Ask students to explain the relationship that exists between two words. Use different types of analogies (e.g., synonym:antonym, cause:effect, part:whole, etc.). Allow students to make their own analogies, and encourage them to share their analogies with one another. Discuss as a class.

Backwards Book Walk

Ask students (independently or in pairs) to look at the conclusion of a nonfiction book or chapter and "read backwards," skimming for headings, captions, italicized/highlighted words, etc. Then ask students to give a title to the text. This activity is meant to help familiarize students with key vocabulary terms.

Choral Reads

There is strength in numbers. As often as possible I lead my ELL students in some sort of choral read – from passages in books to chants to songs to poems. We repeat readings often, and – when students feel comfortable enough to perform on their own – we celebrate what we have learned. I cannot tell you how many silent ELL students I have had in September who were blabber-mouths by December. Choral reads build confidence and allow students to participate in a low-risk environment.

Coded Messages

As students read nonfiction text, ask them to insert "codes," based on their understandings. Students write a check mark above concepts or facts that they already understand, a question mark above concepts or facts that they do not understand, a plus sign above information that is new and an exclamation point above new information that they may find surprising or particularly interesting.

Context Clues

Routinely work with students on how to use their background knowledge to determine unfamiliar word meanings. Appreciate that some words may take multiple exposures before students fully comprehend their meanings.

Hollywood Endings

Read aloud a story to the class without reading the final

three pages of story. Ask students to "write an ending." Another way you can do this is to take a story with a sad ending and ask students to re-write the ending into a happy ending.

Idioms

From a text select some idiomatic expressions (e.g., the test was a piece of cake). Write the idiomatic expression on the whiteboard. Ask students to draw a picture that illustrates the expression and share their pictures. Once students have shared pictures, ask students to predict what the expression means. Write various predictions on whiteboard. Read passage from text that uses idiomatic expression. Allow students to revise their definitions (if necessary) based on the expression's use in the text and write their own sentences that use the expressions. Discuss how students were able to determine meaning of idiomatic expression from the context of the passage (afterward, have students write down three to five additional idiomatic expressions from text. Ask students to repeat steps from before: draw picture of expression, predict expression's meaning, read the text, revise - if necessary - their definitions of each expression and write their own sentences with each expression.

Matching

Prepare a set of cards. Two of the cards within the set can be matched up as a pair. Randomly give a card to each student. Students have to find their partner based on the clues given on the card, and they have to read to each partner the clues that they need. You may vary the difficulty level of the task, based on students' language proficiency levels (e.g., match one picture card to another, match two synonyms, match cause and result, etc.).

Mystery Book

Wrap a book in butcher paper and present to class. Ask students to slowly unwrap the book and try to guess what the book is about (make sure to choose a book with good cover artwork).

Name That Story

As a comprehension activity, read aloud a story without showing students the cover and without telling students the title of the story. Ask students to draw their own covers and provide their own ideas for what would make a good title to the story.

Poetic License

Use poetry to assist in language acquisition. Poetry is a great way to teach ELL students the rhythms of the English language and expose students to a variety of poetry formats. It can also assist in clarifying differences between words that are often confused/misused (e.g., do, due, dew). Some poems that I have created with my students to assist them include basic rhymes (I walked over there, and saw that they're there – a big group of Teddy bears. But when I went there, I saw kids on a chair, and they said that the Teddies were theirs.), Haikus (My mother just sent, a beautiful perfume scent, that cost only three cents.), limericks (There once was a doctor named Lloyd. Many people tried to avoid. He had little patience, for most of his patients, and that's why he's unemployed.), etc.

Read Alouds

Choose a text. Remember that different read alouds require different formats (e.g., reading a magazine article to students is different than reading a chapter book, and reading about the human digestive system is different than reading about child prodigies). Keep in mind that since you are reading the text, you may choose texts that are above your students' level. Before you begin to read the text, announce the name of the book, author and illustrator, and remind students to ask questions if they do not understand something. If you are continuing a book, ask students to review what has happened so far in the text. Establish a warm climate for read alouds. Allow students to get comfortable, whether they are lying on a carpet in front of you or sitting at their desks throughout the classroom. If students want to draw or doodle as you read, let them, as long as they pay attention to the story. On a poster board or piece of butcher paper, create a vocabulary chart of new terms that you encounter in the text. As an extension activity, students may create illustrations to help them remember each term, or they can write sample sentences. If the book has pictures, ask students to describe what is happening in the pictures. Whether or not a book has pictures, you can check for students' understanding by occasionally asking students what is going on in the book and why particular events occur. Another way to keep students involved is to ask them what they think is going to happen next, how the text is similar to their own experiences and what they would do under similar circumstances. As you read, use plenty of expression (e.g., gestures, pacing, intonation). After you read, allow plenty of time for discussion. Allow students to ask questions and make comments about the book. Provide students with time to read on their own, and make sure that they have plenty of interesting materials to choose from (if you are leading a unit on nutrition, it would be a good idea to have a lot of books related to that topic available). It is vital that you read when students read.

Scavenger Hunts

From a text, create a list of unfamiliar vocabulary words that deal with the concept to be studied (e.g., for a unit on measurement: pounds, miles, degrees, minutes, etc.). Take all of the words from the list that can be represented by pictures and objects and add some familiar words that can be represented by pictures or objects until you have a list of approximately 10 represented objects that relate to the topic (e.g., measuring tape, clock, scale, etc.). Have students form small groups of three to four and give each group a scavenger hunt list. Encourage students to use library books, encyclopedias, magazines, textbooks, newspapers, dictionaries, internet resources, junk mail, environmental print and any other resources to find the words on the list.

Stay on Target

One of my ELL students' favorite reading games focuses around high-frequency target vocabulary words. By playing this game on a regular basis (usually as an activity during transitions between lessons), your students will feel better about their familiarity and background knowledge of target vocabulary (e.g., for the target word "through," you'd present students with a list of words and ask students to only circle the word "through" whenever they spotted it: through, though, throb, throw, thought, through, trough, tough, through, threw, throat, throne, thorough, through).

Total Recall

Pair students. One partner recalls a fact about a fable, nursery rhyme, story, etc. from class. The other student must try to identify the title of the fable, nursery rhyme, story, etc. Allow partners opportunities to take turns recalling facts and identifying titles.

And here are some final guidelines to keep in mind when facilitating language development through reading among your ELL students:

Have appropriate expectations for reading comprehension. ELL students will have different levels of understanding depending on whether they are reading for information or for fun, dealing with familiar or unfamiliar topics or authentic or constructed materials. Opportunities for re-reading will also increase students' comprehension levels.

Help your students develop realistic expectations for reading. Learning a second language is not easy. As it is for most language-learning task, misunderstanding the task can lead students to adopt ineffective strategies. Specifically, if students think they are supposed to understand every word in a reading passage, they are likely to become frustrated or to confuse reading with translation. So it is important for teachers to be clear about their expectations for students' reading; and as different cultural groups may have different conceptions of what reading entails, a discussion of what students believe about reading might be helpful. By no means are you lowering expectations. It is important, though, to adjust expectations and allow students time to develop their language skills.

Help students become aware of the background information they need to understand a particular passage. Sometimes teachers do this explicitly, even in the students' native language, by pointing out specific historical events or cultural information that can assist comprehension. A discussion about the topic can remind students of information they already know. Think carefully about what your students already know and what they need to know when reading. If you do not speak the native language(s) of your students, you might want to think about cultural references that may have confused you at one time.

Have students look over the title, headings and any graphics associated with the reading and anticipate what it might be about. An advance organizer in the form of an outline or brief summary is also helpful. By looking at the title, headings, subheadings, graphics and overall physical appearance of a non-fiction text, students will get a good idea of the topic and the kind of text they are about to read. By encouraging students to make predictions about a text, they will begin to develop an important reading strategy that is especially helpful for independent reading.

Have students preview the text by giving them preliminary questions. Students could be asked, for example, to skim through the reading to determine if they are dealing with fiction or nonfiction, how many characters there are, or the setting of the story. Have students review the text several times each time looking for new information. And, by asking students questions that you know they know the answers to, you can build up your ELL students confidence (and willingness to take greater risks).

In the case of content textbooks, have students use end-of-chapter questions as preview questions. Even English-speaking students have difficulty dealing with the amount of information included in today's social studies and science textbooks. By employing the time-honored strategy of using end-of-chapter questions to guide their reading, students can better maneuver the abundance of information. This is probably an essential survival strategy for ELL students who must deal with content assignments and tests at the same time they are learning to read English (e.g., ELL students in the middle and upper grades).

Help students develop effective dictionary strategies and to distinguish "important" from "unimportant" words. Encourage students to guess unknown words from context. After looking up unknown words, students should go back and re-read the whole paragraph before continuing. Many students find it helpful to keep a personal dictionary of words they anticipate needing in conversation or writing or with which they have difficulty.

Ask inference rather than fact-recall questions. Inference questions are as important, and possibly more important, in assessing reading comprehension as they are in determining students' listening comprehension. Since students can easily refer back to a text when reading, it is easy for them to find the answer to a recall question without actually having understood the text – or even the question. Encourage critical thinking skills as much as possible rather than regurgitation of facts.

Provide authentic reading materials as often as possible. The Internet is a great source of authentic reading materials. What did we do before the Internet (scribble on stone tablets)? Take advantage of current technologies and our increasingly interconnected world to help students gain access to a variety of personally relevant reading materials. If technology scares you, ask your ELL students to assist you (as they probably know more about computers than you do, anyway).

Allow ample opportunities for re-reading. Students should be given the opportunity to re-read materials several times. Also, they should be given a purpose each time they read (this can also be called "directed reading").

Take a multimedia approach to reading. Many of today's technologies allow for the development of reading comprehension and listening comprehension simultaneously. Television shows and DVDs can be used with and without captioned subtitles. To help both listening and reading comprehension, students can watch programs with subtitles in English (even if the program is also in English). Recent multimedia technologies allow students to read texts with and without hearing them orally. The combination of audio books and their written counterparts is an excellent low-tech resource for reading, and many children's books are now available in this format.

Writing

ELL students need plenty of time and opportunities to write. They need a purpose to write, such as creating a grocery list or writing a letter to a pen pal. They will write more often and better if they have an audience, such as if they are sharing their writing with classmates or posting a blog on the Internet. Most importantly – and this is starting to sound like a broken record – ELL students need models. When they see writers use writing for real purposes their motivation increases.

If you want to encourage your ELL students to write, you must offer your students a safe and supportive environment that celebrates output. Voluntary sharing, one-on-one conferences (between teacher & student and student & student) and ongoing support throughout the writing workshop are just a few ways good ELL teachers support their students' writing. Feedback, in particular, is one of the most important tools teachers can use to encourage students to write more, paying careful attention to supporting students' composing efforts and guiding them away from "errors," or misuses of English. The most important thing good ELL teachers do to facilitate students' writing efforts is to build a community of writers who feel free to share and celebrate each others' writing while providing one another with helpful feedback for improvement.

Selecting a topic can sometimes be a concern for ELL students. Not all writers find a topic of a personal nature, such as childhood experience, that offers plenty of ideas for writing. Being familiar with a topic is no guarantee of writing ease. The fact that a topic is popular with native English speakers is no guarantee that it will enable ELL students to write.

Cultural differences abound, and teachers need to be aware of what students may or may not feel comfortable writing about. Teachers also need to make sure ELL students understand that different types of writing require different degrees of formality (e.g., text-messaging required much less formal vocabulary than an expository essay). Plagiarism often occurs out of ignorance for accepted norms in American classrooms. Finally, teachers need to ensure that ELL students do not rely too heavily on reference materials, as many ELL students may overuse or misuse dictionaries, thesauruses and encyclopedias.

Since there are so many types of written genres, it is important for teachers to select writing tasks that are connected to ELL students' specific language needs, especially if they have academic purposes for writing. By coordinating reading and writing assignments, students will have models, language structures and ideas that they can apply in their own writing. Keep in mind that there are plenty of opportunities to differentiate writing activities based on individual ELL students' language needs.

Have realistic expectations for writing. New teachers are often surprised and a little dismayed at their ELL students' writing ability. Many ELL students, even those with good oral language proficiency, write at a novice level, since written language must be more precise and organized than oral language. It is also important to remember that students are able to use single words and phrases to participate in conversations, but that written text requires full sentences. Additionally, beginning ELL students often make mistakes in even basic structures, and you should expect that students will continue to make errors even in structures that you have "corrected" before.

Include a variety of types of writing activities. Try to include a variety of structured, communicative, expressive and academic writing activities and help students understand the requirements of each type of writing. Structured writing helps students gain control of new grammatical structures, and expressive writing can help them learn to express their ideas with less hesitation. Communicative and academic writing should be used to help students express their ideas more accurately and precisely.

The type of writing assignment should dictate the type of error correction and teacher response. Explicit corrections are more appropriate for structured and academic writing than for communicative and expressive writing, but it is always more important to respond to the students' ideas. Unfortunately, it is not always easy to figure out what a student is trying to say. In that case, mark the specific sentences and tell the student that you don't understand. This is where peer conferencing can be particularly helpful.

Help your students develop realistic expectations about writing. Since students have more time when they write than when they speak, they are going to be even more likely to try to translate from their native language. Try to discourage translation by telling students to think in the new language and reminding them that they will have opportunities to revise. They should understand that the ideas that they will be able to express in the new language will not be as sophisticated as the ideas they can express in their first language.

Help your students clarify their thoughts before writing. Encourage students to brainstorm, outline and plan their writing before they get started. Just as with reading, it is a good idea to include pre-writing activities to remind students of information they already know that might be useful for a particular assignment.

Point out specific conventions of different writing genres. Do not assume that ELL students will know what to include in their writing, and give them clear guidelines about necessary components. For example, if students need to write an argumentative essay in English, tell them it will need an introductory paragraph with a statement or thesis, several arguments and a concluding paragraph that takes their analysis a step beyond their original thesis. It would be a good idea to show them several samples of argumentative essays, as well as a clear rubric, so that they can see concrete examples of the type of writing you are assigning and your expectations of their writing. You may also want to remind them of specific vocabulary words and structures that may be useful in their writing.

Try group writing. We tend to associate group work with oral activities rather than written ones, but partner/

small-group writing activities can also be effective. Group interaction and negotiation helps ELL students determine what they want to say and to phrase their ideas more comprehensibly.

Use technology as an asset. Electronic writing (e.g., emails, text messaging, etc.) can make writing more motivating and even fun for students. By communicating with a real person (teachers, their classmates, native-speaking peers) they have an authentic reason to write.

Coordinate writing assignments with the materials students are reading and content material they are learning. Due to differences in writing conventions or limited literacy in their native language, many ELL students will have little idea of how a written text should be organized. Having students read authentic texts with a similar structure gives students a model for their work. In addition, by having students write about content that they have learned, they get practice with the kind of writing they will need in academic classes.

Give students guide questions. Another way to help

students organize their ideas into a particular writing format is to guide them through the writing with targeted questions. When they have answered the questions, they will have produced a draft of the assignment.

Help students develop effective dictionary (and other reference books) strategies. Have a class discussion about how to use dictionaries and other writing strategies.

Encourage revision. Encourage students to think of writing as a process and build revision into all writing assignments.

Be aware of the role of affect in writing. Many people feel uncomfortable writing in their native language, and when writing in a second language they must deal with the additional problem of their limited language proficiency. Encourage students to stop and brainstorm or to break the writing task down into manageable parts, especially if they experience writer's block. Unfortunately, teachers sometimes add to their students' writing anxiety. Avoid telling students that a particular writing assignment or type of writing is hard, and try to correct errors gently.

Make writing fun. I love writing. I believe the reason a lot of students hate writing is because most adults hate writing. The reason a lot of adults hate writing is because they were taught how to write using five-paragraph essays. Now, I have nothing against five-paragraph essays, but writing can be so much more. Writing can be poetry. Writing can be creating newspaper ads. There are endless ways ELL teachers may incorporate writing throughout the day in fun and meaningful ways. Here is a sampling of some of my favorites:

Brochures

As a comprehension activity, encourage students to create brochures that tell others about highlights of what they have read (in the case of a storybook) or learned (e.g., place value, hardness of rocks, American history, etc.). You may also encourage students to create brochures in native language as well as English.

Comic Strip Sequencing

Select cartoons with a very clear and predictable pattern of events. Eliminate the dialogue in the discussion bubbles, and allow students to work in pairs to develop new dialogue to accompany the action.

Dialogue Journals

Create open-ended sentences and topics of general interest to students (e.g., In the summer I like to…, If I could eat lunch with anyone, it would be with…, etc.). After student writes an entry, you should write a brief, positive response in the margin of the entry to encourage further writing by the student.

Fill-in-the-Blanks

Prepare a set of cards. Two of the cards within the set can be matched up as a pair. One card is the opening line from a story read in class, and the other is the closing line from a story read in class. Randomly give a card to each student. Students have to find a partner based on the clues given on the card. It does not matter if students find the matching opening and closing lines from a story. The two partners now have to create a story that links the beginning with the ending.

Flannel Board Story

Tell a story using a flannel board and flannel cut-out characters (if you don't have a flannel board/cut-out characters, then use a white board and cardboard cut-out characters). As you tell the story, students place each character cut-out on the board. Ask students to identify the characters in a variety of ways, such as pointing and providing short answers. Ask students to retell the story or create a new story using the same characters. Ask them to write down their story to share with the class later, or students can write about topics based on the discussion by drawing, labeling characters and using short sentences. Please note: you can use this activity across subject areas (e.g., instead of a story, you could present students with concepts such as counting, addition and subtraction).

Found Poems
Select a reading that is short, rich in language and has a distinct message to communicate. Give each student a copy of the reading. Read aloud the piece to the class, asking students to circle words or phrases that they particularly like. In small groups, students create a Found Poem using all the words and phrases they circled (Found Poems are sort of like collages – students create a new text by reordering items from another text; a good example can be found in *The Stinky Cheese Man*

and Other Fairly Stupid Tales by Jon Scieszka, as the Giant takes common storybook phrases and puts them together in his own order, starting with "And they lived happily ever after"). Each group reads aloud their Found Poem chorally to the class.

Golden Books
While many ELL students may have difficulties writing in English, they may be proficient writers in their native language. Encourage students to write books in their native languages, and – as the year progresses and their English improves – ask them to write the English translation of their stories in the books. I call these "golden books" because they are especially helpful in encouraging parents to read and write with their children (in my experience, while many ELL parents may not be able to read and write in English, they can read and write in their native languages).

Guessing Game
Place an object inside a bag and ask students to stick their arms inside. Hold the bag so that students may not see the object. Each student takes a turn and comes up

with a descriptive word about the object. Other students create a word list and, based on descriptors, guess what the object is. Class may create a story based on the object and their guesses.

Interactive Word Walls

Create a bulletin board that is divided into areas for different letters of the alphabet. On sentence strips, write new vocabulary words from the text and pin them on to the interactive word wall. Introduce the word wall to students and encourage them to utilize the word wall when they are writing. As the interactive word wall will be used as an on-going resource, encourage the class to add new vocabulary words to the word wall that they encounter in the text. Students may also keep a "file" of their own vocabulary cards for their groups for easier access. As an extension activity, students may illustrate words or write additional information about words on the back of their cards (e.g., variations of word, synonyms, sample sentences, etc.). As the word wall is meant to be interactive, it is important that the class reviews the wall frequently during the unit. Refer to the word wall frequently. The interactive word wall is meant as an additional reference for students to use in their writing and understanding of text. Facilitate daily experiences with the word wall, such as chanting the words, asking students to ask questions to try to guess a word that you are thinking of, allowing students to create sentences with various words, etc.

K-W-L+

Choose a nonfiction text and select a key topic to be covered in that text. Provide each student with his or her own K-W-L Plus strategy sheet. Ask students to brainstorm what they know about the topic ("K"). Record student responses on the whiteboard while students record their responses on their strategy sheets. As students provide ideas, ask them questions such as "Where did you learn that?" and "How might you prove it?" Encourage students to review the completed column of information they know about the topic and try to place the different types of information into categories. If students have initial difficulty identifying categories, suggest a couple of categories by relating what students will be reading to other topics previously covered in class. While students brainstorm different pieces and categories of information they know about the topic, record any areas of interest students want to know about but are uncertain about ("W"). Ask students to record any questions they want answered before they read. Allow students to read the text. For particularly difficult texts, preview the text with students and/or allow students to read the texts in parts. Following students' reading of the text, ask students to write the answers to their questions ("L"). Discuss answers as a class, recording student responses on the whiteboard. Ask students to share questions they had that were not answered by the text or any new questions they developed while reading. Record these questions ("+") and discuss where students may be able to obtain answers to these questions.

Labeling

Let your ELL students "identify" the room by creating labels for various objects (e.g., whiteboard, desk, clock, etc.). Encourage students to label in native languages as well as in English.

Paint Strip Ladders

Hand students each a paint strip sample (you can get

these from any paint store). Students each write a "dull" word in the box with the dull color on the left hand side of the strip. Writing left to write, students write a "richer" word in each box (e.g., pretty => beautiful => gorgeous => stunning). Encourage students to write poems, using richer vocabulary.

Pantomime
Prepare six to eight short sentences describing a sequence of actions in a specific context. Then collect or create visuals and props to accompany each action. Act out the sentences using visuals and props while clearly saying the sentences. Students respond in pantomime, first in groups and then on their own. Stop modeling the actions and ask students to orally respond to the sentences. Students now imitate the sentences as well as the actions. Finally, students write the actions and read their scripts aloud. For example, you could review what students are to do when they come to class: 1. I enter the room; 2. I go to my seat; 3. I sit down; 4. I take out my book; 5. I take out my pencil; 6. I greet my teacher.

Pattern Poems

Create a format of a poem (e.g., haiku, cinquain, acrostic, etc.). The pattern can be based on a piece of literature that the students have read in class. Model writing a poem in that format, using student input (reinforcing students' listening and speaking skills). Students use the format and any target vocabulary to create their own poems (e.g., I used to be fat, but now I'm skinny. I used to be ____, but now I'm ____).

Personal Vocabulary Journals

Make personal vocabulary journals with students for each curricular area. One easy approach is to have students staple 10-15 sheets of lined paper between two pieces of construction paper that will serve as the personal vocabulary journal's cover. Ask students to write their names and the title of the curricular area (e.g., "mathematics vocabulary journal") on their personal vocabulary journal covers. Personal vocabulary journals are used as an on-going activity. To that end, model various types of vocabulary journal activities that students can perform before, during and after their reading. Some examples of activities include taking notes, drawing diagrams, listing new vocabulary words, writing personal reflections and using illustrations to remember key concepts. Ask students to turn-in their personal vocabulary journals and review their notes and questions. Provide feedback where necessary.

Possible Sentences

Write key vocabulary terms from the text on the whiteboard. Pronounce each word, and make sure that each word can be defined by using the text. Ask students to select pairs of words from the list. For each pair, have students write a sentence that they think might appear in the text. Ask student volunteers to write their sentences on the board, underlining the words the students have included from the list. Discuss sentences. Ask if anyone disagrees with any of the sentences and have students read the text on their own to verify the accuracy of their sentences. Discuss sentences again as a class. Have students evaluate sentences for accuracy, and ask students to make any changes they wish. Ask students to create additional sentences based on information from the text. Encourage students to record their sentences in their notebooks for further study.

Semantic Mapping

Select a key word or concept and enclose the word in a box in the center of the board or overhead. Ask students to form small groups and brainstorm words related to the key word or concept. List students' suggested words on the board or overhead and group into broad categories. Ask students to name categories and suggest additional ones. Discuss semantic map as a class. For further clarification, connect categories with lines to the key word or concept. Relationship words may be written on the lines.

Signal Words

Create a list of words and phrases that "signal" the four types of text structures: compare/contrast, cause/effect, sequence/order and description/list. For example, you may brainstorm and create a classroom poster for signal words that compare (e.g., like, also, similarly, etc.) and contrast (e.g., on the other hand, but, however, etc.) two or more things. Encourage students to refer to their signal word posters when they write.

Sound Effects

Play different recorded sounds from the environment aloud on an audiotape. Students listen to the sounds and identify them by discussing with a partner. Partners then draw and/or write the word. Students can also create sounds and ask classmates to guess what each sound is.

Thank-You Cards

One way to promote generosity among students and develop language is to encourage students to write thank-you cards to one another, their teachers, other school employees and family members. Show your ELL students some of the purposes of writing and instantly inspire them by providing them with an audience for their new English writing skills.

Vocabulary Cards

Give students "vocabulary card" index cards in which students use illustrations to show their understanding of a vocabulary word. Ask students to write the word on one side of the card. On the other side of the card, students divide their cards into four quadrants: in the upper left-hand quadrant they write the definition of the word; in the lower left-hand quadrant they write examples of the word; in the upper right-hand quadrant they write characteristics of the word; and in the lower right-hand corner of the card they write non-examples of the word. So, if the word is "mammals," the upper left-hand corner of a student's card may read:

Definition: a member of a class of higher vertebrates

The upper right-hand corner of the card may look like this:

Characteristics:
- warm-blooded
- babies are born live (no eggs)
- have fur
- have a backbone

In the lower left-hand corner of the card, a student may write:

Examples:
- humans

- rabbits
- monkeys
- dogs
- cats

And the lower right-hand corner of the card may contain information like this:

Non-Examples:
- fish
- snakes
- ants
- lizards
- turtles

Word Riddles

From a text, choose a key concept (e.g., "space"), and ask students to brainstorm a list of words (e.g., "solar system," "sun," "moon," "stars," "Earth," etc.) related to the key concept. Select a word from the list (e.g., "star"). Drop the first letter(s) from the word to get a shortened version ("star" - "s" = "tar") and ask students to brainstorm a list of words that begin the way the shortened version begins (e.g., target, tarantula, tartar sauce, tardy, Tarzan, tarp, etc.). Select a word from this list of words and put back the first letter that was initially dropped (e.g., stardy, starget, Starzan). This new "word" will serve as the answer to a riddle. As a class create a riddle question that highlights this word as an answer (e.g., What do you call a man who swings from planet to planet? "Starzan."). Ask students to read text and find more words to use for riddles (or select 2-5 additional key words from the text). Encourage students to work with partners and create riddles on their own. Share riddles as a class.

Wordtoons
Developed by Wayne Logue (www.wordtoons.com), Wordtoons are one of my favorite ways to encourage students to write. Wayne shows teachers how to turn high-frequency vocabulary words into cartoons. It is a wonderful way to get students excited about writing.

Word Walls/Word Banks
Post a bulletin board with the alphabet, and ask students

to add key, high-frequency words on index cards whenever they find the words useful. Ask students to write words in their own private word banks (these can be journals, note cards or papers taped to the tops of their desks for quick reference). Students then use these words to create sentences and prepare for reading.

World Map Facts
Create a bulletin board or learning center with a world map. Students use thumbtacks or markers to highlight different countries. For each country students highlight, they fill out index cards with information they know about that country and place them in a basket. Postcards, pictures and small objects may also be placed in each country's basket. You can incorporate this activity into daily meeting as an opportunity for students to present what they know about a country to the entire class.

Final Thoughts

It is not easy learning a second language.

Learning a second language can be frustrating, debilitating and humbling. Many ELL students can feel sad, lonely and angry. They may lose sleep, experience headaches and suffer from depression. Your role as an ELL teacher is to provide a positive, safe environment that promotes language acquisition.

Keep the following tips in mind:

1. Keep it simple. Think of your dirty garage: it is much easier to motivate yourself to clean one corner at a time than to comprehend the immensity of a project. Learning English is the same. It is easier to think of it in bite-size chunks.
2. Use a variety of visual, auditory and kinesthetic strategies to connect with students. Check for understanding frequently, and don't fall into the "Does everybody understand?" trap, as your students will most likely just nod their heads. Challenge students to demonstrate understanding in a variety of ways.
3. Make sure your activities touch upon standards. Any good administrator will support you, as long as there is an educational rationale behind what you do.
4. Slow down. Remember: Rome wasn't built in a day.
5. Use songs, chants and games as 2-3 min. transitional activities to keep students' attention during "standards-based" lessons. The goal is to promote critical thinking skills throughout the day.
6. Encourage movement. The brain likes movement - and we want concepts to stick!

7. Familiarize yourself with students' native cultures and foster understanding among students about common practices in America.

8. Avoid complex sentences and the passive voice.

9. Use student translators: when you are unable to translate a message, have student translators translate your message so it is understandable.

10. Use as many non-verbal clues as possible (provide "comprehensible input" in the form of gestures, visuals, etc.).

11. Allow plenty of wait time for student responses.

12. Focus on communication, not "correcting" students "errors."

13. Praise student efforts. Encourage often.

14. Be patient.

15. Smile, and have fun, for goodness sake!

NOTES

Invest In Danny's Top-Selling Book!

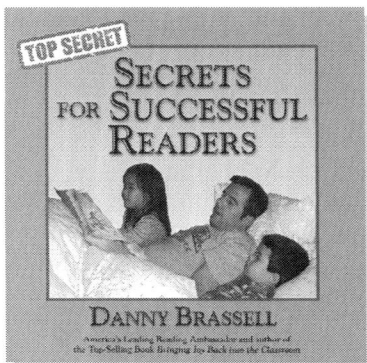

Secrets for Successful Readers

What Every Parent & Teacher Needs to Know to Inspire Children to Love Reading & Achieve More

$19.97

Learn how to excite children about learning, attract students to a variety of reading materials, find great books, build solid literacy foundations to achieve greater results and make reading fun.

Special Quantity Discounts

10-20 Books	$16.00 each
21-99 Books	$15.00 each
100-499 Books	$12.00 each
500-999 Books	$10.00 each
1,000+ Books	$8.00 each

www.dannybrassell.com

Burnt out? Frustrated by the Latest Federal, State & Local Mandates and Standards? Let Danny Provide You with Caffeine for Your Soul!

WHETHER YOU ARE A TEACHER SEARCHING FOR WAYS to meet the needs of English language learners or a principal trying to boost employee morale and effectiveness, Danny's trainings have a lasting impact on your audience. You'll find how learning, disguised as play, will have a dramatic effect on your long-term results. In this "Educator Empowerment Series" package, you'll receive **THREE** of Danny's most acclaimed keynotes and seminars, including:

• **Bringing Joy Back Into the Classroom** The standardized testing craze has terrified students and led many great teachers to quit. In this popular keynote Danny reminds educators of their importance in the every day development of children.

• **A Baker's Dozen of Lessons Learned from the Teaching Trenches** Join Danny in this fast-paced, humorous and motivational keynote as he shares his own trials and tribulations in the classroom as well as why he loves to teach. You'll learn his secret to good teaching and leave feeling invigorated.

• **Dare to Differentiate: 50 Terrific Teacher Tricks** In this eye-opening session Danny shares 50 tricks successful teachers use to stimulate students' interest in learning, and you'll learn how to incorporate standards by using fun songs, games and activities in your classroom.

Special Only $39.97 Reg. Price! $49.97

To place an Order, visit www.dannybrassell.com, or call (310) 872-9089

www.dannybrassell.com